Ages
5~7

SECTION
1

The Snail and the Whale

SECTION
6

Get writing

SECTION
7

Assessment

PAGE
1

Read & Respond

Ages
5–7

Author: Jean Evans

Commissioning Editor: Rachel Mackinnon

Editor: Carole Sunderland

Assistant Editor: Jo Kemp

Series Designer: Anna Oliwa

Designer: Dan Prescott

Illustrations: Paul Hutchinson

Text © 2011, Jean Evans © 2011, Scholastic Ltd

Designed using Adobe InDesign

Published by Scholastic Ltd,
Book End, Range Road, Witney,
Oxfordshire OX29 0YD
www.scholastic.co.uk

Printed by Bell & Bain
1 2 3 4 5 6 7 8 9   1 2 3 4 5 6 7 8 9 0

British Library Cataloguing-in-Publication Data
A catalogue record for this book is available from
the British Library.
ISBN 978-1407-12703-3

Acknowledgements

The publishers gratefully acknowledge permission to reproduce the following copyright material: **Macmillan Children's Books** for the use of the cover, text and illustrations from *The Snail and the Whale* by Julia Donaldson and Axel Scheffler. Text © 2003 Julia Donaldson. Illustrations © 2003, Axel Scheffler (2003, Macmillan Children's Books).
Every effort has been made to trace copyright holders for the works reproduced in this book, and the publishers apologise for any inadvertent omissions.

The Snail and the Whale

About the book

The Snail and the Whale tells the heart-warming story of a tiny snail with an *itchy foot* who longs to go sailing and discover the world. A message she leaves on a rock is read by a humpback whale who beckons the tiny snail to *'Come sail'*. However, their fantastic journey is interrupted when the whale becomes beached. Now the tiny snail must come to the aid of her huge new friend. She summons help from schoolchildren and firemen who keep the rapidly dehydrating whale cool until the tide comes in. The happy ending sees the snail and the whale set sail once more, this time with the other snails, the *flock on the rock*.

Strong characters abound in Julia Donaldson's books, and becoming familiar with what makes them so memorable supports young writers as they develop their own characters. As children share the adventures of this unlikely partnership, they will consider the importance of good friendships, especially if linked to other traditional tales such as 'The Lion and the Mouse'.

Shared reading of the text provides excellent opportunities for teaching and applying Key Stage 1 skills at word and text level. Children are encouraged to appreciate the effects of rich patterned language, rhyme and repetition as they join in with reading, clap word rhythms and invent their own rhymes. They sequence events in the story, for example, by following the journey of the snail and the whale, before writing their own versions. Also included are opportunities for exploring detail in the illustrations and for discussing how these extend and enhance the text.

About the author and illustrator

Julia Donaldson is an extremely popular children's author with a natural ability to understand children's innermost thoughts and imaginative worlds. Her musical background, coupled with her wonderful rhyme and language skills, led to a career in singing and songwriting, mainly for BBC children's television. One of her television songs, 'A Squash and a Squeeze', was made into a book in 1993, with quirky illustrations by Axel Scheffler.

Of all Julia's characters, perhaps the favourite is *The Gruffalo*, whose inspiration has roots in Chinese folklore. *The Gruffalo* has also been released in the form of audio books, toys and musical CDs and has toured as a musical stage play.

Axel Scheffler has collaborated on picture books with Julia since the publication of *A Squash and a Squeeze*, but is also the best-selling illustrator of books such as *The Bedtime Bear* and *The Tickle Book*. His distinctive characters and humorous details enhance Julia Donaldson's unique verse perfectly. Other popular characters published by this successful partnership include *Tiddler, Stick Man* and *Tabby McTat*.

Facts and figures
The Snail and the Whale
Author: Julia Donaldson
Illustrator: Axel Scheffler
First published: 2003 by Macmillan Children's Books.
Awards: Winner of Books Trust Early Years Award 2004 for best pre-school book, winner of Blue Peter Children's Book Prize 2005 for best illustrated book to read aloud, winner of the Giverny Award for Children's Science Picture Books 2007.

Guided reading

Introducing the book

Show the front cover of the book. Read the title and ask: *Can we tell from the title who the main characters might be? What do you notice about the words 'snail' and 'whale'? What might this tell us about the way the story is told?* (It might be a rhyming story.)

Draw attention to the names 'Julia Donaldson' and 'Axel Scheffler'. Ask if the children have heard of either of them. Establish who is the author and who is the illustrator of the book. (You can find out more about them in Section 1.) Encourage the children to name some other titles that they have read by Julia Donaldson. Discuss what they know about her style, for example, that the stories are often funny and usually in rhyme.

Look at the illustration of the monkey on the back cover, especially its facial expression. Ask the children if this distinctive style reminds them of the work of Axel Scheffler in any other books.

Explore the illustrations on the front and back covers together. Look at the image of the whale in the ocean and the background landscape. Ask: *Can you spot the two main characters mentioned in the title? Where do you think they might be going? What can you tell about the possible setting of the story?* Prompt the children to look for visual clues about this landscape, for example, the palm trees, lizard, parrot, toucan and monkey indicate that it is a tropical country, perhaps an island.

Turn to the back cover and read the short blurb. Ask: *What more can you learn about the appearance of one of the main characters from this blurb?* (It is a tiny sea snail.) *What might be different about this snail?* (She longs to sail.) *Do you know if it is a boy or girl snail? Can you find any more evidence that the story is in rhyme? What do you think the story might be about after reading this blurb?*

Initial reading

Ensure that the first reading is as clear, expressive and engaging as possible. Encourage participation by asking the children to join in with predictable,

patterned language, for example, *This is the tale of the tiny snail / And a great big, grey-blue humpback whale.* Vary vocal tone to build up mood and atmosphere, for example, saying *sharks* loudly and with a menacing expression. Emphasise words such as *shooting stars and enormous waves* with gestures and by raising and lowering your voice. Use actions, for example, making fingers 'crawl' on the back of a hand to demonstrate the tiny snails crawling onto the whale's tail.

As you read, track the text, left to right, word by word, with a finger or pointer. Pause at significant points to ask the children what they think will happen next or to predict a word or phrase, for example, *Who do you think will read the snail's trail asking for a lift? Where do you think the whale will take the snail?*

Check understanding through appropriate comments and queries. Ask, for example, *Why do you think the snail had an 'itchy foot'? What do you think this expression means? What do you already know about the snail? Does this knowledge help you with these questions?*

Explain language such as *hitch a lift, coral caves, earsplitting* and *frolicked*, using activities as necessary to aid understanding. For example, provide a blackboard and chalk so that the children can pretend to be the snail writing her message, *'Lift wanted around the world'*, in a *silvery trail* on the rock. Demonstrate the meaning of *hitch a lift* with a thumb. Invite the children to pretend to be waves dancing, introducing the word 'frolic' afterwards by saying, for example, *You really captured the playful way that waves frolic and dance in the ocean.*

Encourage the children to consider how characters are feeling as the story progresses. Ask: *Have you ever longed to do something different? What did you want to do? Have you ever felt small in a huge open space or upset by a loud noise?* Always be prepared to follow the children's comments, interests and ideas when you ask these questions, and encourage respect for differing opinions and aspirations.

Draw attention to the rich and detailed illustrations and discuss how they enhance the story. For example, ask about the busy opening harbour scene: *How can you tell this is a harbour? Why do you think there is a lighthouse on the harbour wall? What things have been washed in by the tide? How can you tell that the sea covers all of the rocks when the tide comes in? What is the purpose of the cranes? Where might the oil drums have come from?*

The trail of the snail

Before any subsequent reading, observe some snails. Discuss the trails that they leave as they slide along. Focus on the importance of the tiny snail's *silvery trail* and how this natural feature shapes the story. Ask: *How does the tiny snail use her trail to communicate? Where does she write her two messages?* (On the black rock and on the school blackboard.) *What two messages does she leave? (Lift wanted around the world* and *Save the whale.) Who responds to her trails?* (The humpback whale and the schoolchildren.) *Why are the letters in the trails connected to one another and joined to the other words in a continuous line?*

Peril and adventure

Read the story together and discuss how the author and illustrator make the story more exciting, for example, with *enormous waves,* roaring speedboats, sharks with *hideous toothy grins* and frightening storms. Talk about how the snail *felt helpless and terribly small* when the whale lay moaning on the beach. Ask the children how they would feel in this situation.

Save the whale

Read about events that led to the whale becoming marooned on the beach. Discuss how his friend was able to get help for him. Talk about the role played by the tiny snail, the children and the firemen in keeping the whale cool. Ask: *What happened to the whale when the tide came in? What would you do if you ever came across a beached whale?*

Rhyme for a reason

Focus on the importance of rhyme and rhythm in the book. Read through the first page, emphasising the rhyming word at the end of each line. Read it again, inviting the children to join in with the rhyming words. Read a rhyming couplet and then repeat it, this time changing the order of the words so that it no longer rhymes. So, for example, read *Sometimes sunny and blue and warm, Sometimes filled with a thunderstorm,* then say, 'Sometimes warm and blue and sunny, Sometimes filled with a thunderstorm'. Ask: *Which version rhymes? Which one do you think sounds best?*

Popular patterns

Draw attention to the way that the words *This is the…* or *These are the…* are consistently used to move the story along by introducing characters or objects. Talk about how descriptive words often follow to form a satisfying rhythmical sentence, for example, *These are the waves that arched and crashed, That foamed and frolicked and sprayed and splashed.* Change the sentence to 'These are the arching, crashing, foaming, splashing, frolicking waves'. Ask the children what they notice. (The meaning is the same but the sentence is cluttered and the lilting rhythm has gone.) Read the traditional rhyme 'This is the House that Jack Built' and make similar comparisons about moving events along with a regular rhythm.

Book review

To conclude, invite the children to reconsider their original impressions of the book. Encourage them to voice their opinions with confidence and clarity, making direct references to the text wherever possible. Ask: *Do you still feel the same about this story or have your opinions changed since our first reading? Why do you feel different now? What have you discovered that is new? Do you think the story works well because it uses rhyme*

Guided reading

and pattern or do you think it could be improved in another way? Have your opinions changed about the illustrations now that you have explored them in detail? What was your favourite part of the story? Was there any part of the story that you did not enjoy? Do you think the most important character is the snail or the whale, or do you think they are equally important? Is there anything that you particularly liked or disliked about each of these characters? Did your feelings towards them change at different points in the story? How do you feel about the story ending?

Shared reading

Extract 1

● Display the extract and discuss the information it contains. Ask: *What do the opening two lines tell us? Can we identify the main characters? Do we know where the story is set? Does the last sentence tell us what might happen next?*

● Draw attention to the punctuation and ask: *How can we tell when the snail is speaking? Why does the author use exclamation marks in the snail's speech?*

● Ask a child to highlight, in the first sentence, the adjectives describing the two main characters. (*Tiny* and *great big, blue-grey humpback*.) Underline *as black as soot* and ask the children if this is a good way to describe the rock. Suggest that they think of similar ways to describe the shells and seaweed that cover it, for example, 'as hard as stone', 'as smooth as silk'. Introduce the word 'simile' if the children are ready.

● Circle and discuss the effectiveness of 'movement' words such as *slithered, gazed, sniffed* and *sighed*. Demonstrate the need to move your eyes in a concentrated way to gaze, to wrinkle your nose to sniff and to lift your shoulders to let out a sigh.

● Identify rhyming words and ask the children what they notice about their position on each line. Discuss how the spelling of rhyming sounds can be the same or different.

Extract 2

● Read this extract together and discuss the content. Ask: *How did the whale get into difficulties? What upset him? What do you think will happen to him?*

● Underline *But then* and talk about how the words indicate a change in direction of the story. Ask the children for other connectives to join two different events in a story and imply that something new is about to happen, for example, 'All too soon…' and 'Suddenly…'.

● Read the description of the movement of the speedboats. Discuss how the author uses words such as *zigging and zooming* and *running a race*. Ask: *What do these words tell us about the direction of the speedboats? Are the speedboats really 'running a race'? Why do you think the author has said this?* Draw attention to the alliteration and its effect.

Extract 3

● Read this extract together. Encourage the children to read high frequency words on sight and to recognise alternative ways of spelling graphemes, for example, 'frail' and 'tale'.

● Circle adjectives such as *shimmering, looping* and *silvery*. Explore their effectiveness by trying out alternatives with similar meanings to see if they improve the descriptions.

● To establish whether this is a good ending, begin by discussing the content of the extract. Ask: *What do we know about the story from this extract? Do you think the snail and the whale told their tale well? What did the other snails do after they heard it?*

● Suggest that by summing up the story in her ending, the author makes the story seem complete. Ask: *Do you like this ending? How does it leave you feeling? When the other snails set sail as well, do you think that this might lead to another adventure?*

Extract 1

This is a tale of a tiny snail
And a great big, grey-blue humpback whale.

This is a rock as black as soot,
And this is a snail with an itchy foot.

The sea snail slithered all over the rock
And gazed at the sea and the ships in the dock.
And as she gazed she sniffed and sighed.
"The sea is deep and the world is wide!
How I long to sail!"
Said the tiny snail.

SCHOLASTIC
www.scholastic.co.uk

Extract 2

But then came the day
The whale lost his way…

These are the speedboats, running a race,
Zigging and zooming all over the place,
Upsetting the whale with their earsplitting roar,
Making him swim too close to the shore.

This is the tide, slipping away…
And this is the whale lying beached in a bay.

Extract 3

And the whale and the snail

Told their wonderful tale

Of shimmering ice and coral caves,

And shooting stars and enormous waves,

And of how the snail, so small and frail,

With her looping, curling, silvery trail,

Saved the life of the humpback whale.

Then the humpback whale

Held out his tail

And on crawled snail after snail after snail.

And they sang to the sea as they all set sail

On the tail of the grey-blue humpback whale.

Plot, character and setting

What an adventure!

Objective: To consider how mood and atmosphere are created in live and recorded performances.
What you need: Copies of *The Snail and the Whale*, video recording equipment, everyday sound-making items such as small pebbles, sand, plastic bottles and metal trays, beach toys.
Cross-curricular links: PSHE, drama.

What to do
● After reading the story, invite the children to imagine that they are playing on one of the beach settings in the book on a sunny day.
● Discuss sounds that might be heard, such as waves gently rolling or seagulls calling. Now imagine the same beach during a heavy storm. Would the sounds be the same?
● Experiment with everyday objects to create beach sounds, for example, dropping pebbles onto a metal tray or swishing water in a bottle.

● In groups, create short scenarios about playing on a sunny beach and becoming caught in a storm. Provide appropriate resources to record these and ask the children to allocate roles, for example, sound engineers, directors, actors.
● Put on live performances. Follow this by watching their associated video recordings. Discuss whether mood and atmosphere have been successfully created in both.

Differentiation
For older/more confident learners: Ask children to introduce characters from *The Snail and the Whale* into their dramatisations.
For younger/less confident learners: Concentrate on acting out events and join the children, in role, to talk through the action, for example, 'Those black clouds make me shiver. Maybe a storm is coming.'

When did that happen?

Objective: To identify the main events and characters in stories and find specific information in simple texts.
What you need: Copies of *The Snail and the Whale*, photocopiable page 15, scissors.
Cross-curricular link: Mathematics.

What to do
● Read the story. Discuss what happens at the beginning, middle and end of the story.
● Display the photocopiable sheet and read it together. Ask whether the children think that these sentences tell the story in the correct order.
● Highlight suitable sentences to represent the beginning and ending of the story.
● Put the children into pairs. Ask each pair to cut out and arrange the sentences from the photocopiable sheet in their chosen order.
● Bring the class together to share their sequences.

Were many in the same order? Which is the most accurate sequence? (Suggested sequence is 4, 7, 3, 1, 9, 6, 2, 8, 5.)
● Number the remaining sentences in the order in which these events occur.
● Read the story together in this new order and make adjustments until the children are satisfied.

Differentiation
For older/more confident learners: Ask pairs of children to make up sentences on paper strips to create similar 'Tell the story' puzzles. They should then swap puzzles with another pair and try to reorder the sentences to make the story.
For younger/less confident learners: Create a simplified version of the photocopiable sheet with short sentences related to the beginning, middle and end of the story.

Plot, character and setting

The snail with the itchy foot

Objective: To experiment with and build new stores of words to communicate in different contexts.
What you need: Copies of *The Snail and the Whale*, photocopiable page 16, colouring pencils/pens, scissors, glue.
Cross-curricular link: Science.

What to do
● Display the photocopiable sheet and focus initially on labelling the parts of a snail. Talk about how a snail has one muscular foot that it uses to move along. Explain the purpose of tentacles.
● Explore the illustrations on the second double-page spread of the story and compare the features of the sea snails with snails the children have seen.
● Discuss the rest of the photocopiable sheet, considering what the words tell us about the tiny snail's character.
● Talk about the meaning of *itchy foot*, explaining that people with 'itchy feet' are usually eager to do something else. Think of alternative words for 'itchy feet', for example, 'restless', 'discontented'.
● Introduce a group hot-seating activity with children taking on the role of the snail while others ask about how she is feeling, her greatest wish and so on.
● Provide each child with the photocopiable sheet to complete.
● Bring the class together and invite children to show their labelled pictures and read out their sentences. Decide which ones use the most appropriate words to describe the tiny snail.

Differentiation
For older/more confident learners: Ask children to write a short paragraph about the character and appearance of the tiny snail using some of the new words they have discovered.
For younger/less confident learners: Modify the photocopiable sheet to include words that challenge individuals at an appropriate level.

Picture this

Objective: To create short, simple texts on paper and on screen that combine words with images (and sounds).
What you need: Copies of *The Snail and the Whale,* large sheets of card, collage materials, paint, computer access.
Cross-curricular link: Art and design.

What to do
● Together, explore the illustrations depicting different settings in the story and read the accompanying text.
● Make a class list of setting headings and add notes alongside, for example, 'The harbour – big ships, jetty, lighthouse, cliffs, crane'.
● Divide the children into groups. Invite each group to choose and then make a large picture of one of the settings, referring to the book illustration and using the creative materials provided.
● Ask the groups to invent captions to describe their finished pictures, for example, 'This far-off land has a huge volcano and golden beaches. Monkeys, turtles and parrots live here.'
● Ask the children to write or type and print their captions to attach to their creative work.
● Bring the class together to share pictures and read captions. Display the pictures along the wall in the order they appear in the story.

Differentiation
For older/more confident learners: Invite the children to create simple computer images of the settings, with added captions and sound effects, such as seagulls and wind.
For younger/less confident learners: Ask the children to paint setting pictures based on short captions, for example, 'Here is the black rock', 'Here is the big bay'.

Plot, character and setting

The journey

> **Objective:** To use planning to establish clear sections for writing.
> **What you need:** Copies of *The Snail and the Whale*, large sheets of paper, coloured pens, photocopiable page 17.
> **Cross-curricular links:** Geography, mathematics.

What to do
● Talk about maps and how they are used to plot journeys. Explain that you would like the children to find a way of plotting the journey that the snail and the whale took.
● Draw a circle with a dot at the top to represent the *smooth black rock*. Write the children's suggestions for places visited by the snail and the whale around the circle, joining each one with an arrow. Follow the arrows around the route, reading the names of places and starting and finishing at the black rock.

● Divide the children into groups and ask each group to draw a similar journey map on a large sheet of paper with key settings linked by arrows.
● Share and discuss the maps as a class before providing each child with the photocopiable sheet to complete.
● Use the group and individual work to support children's written plans before they tell or write their own versions of the story.

> **Differentiation**
> **For older/more confident learners:** Invite the children to make up a story about a journey, using the different places visited to form the scaffolding of their plan.
> **For younger/less confident learners:** Make a big 'journey map' on the floor using carpet squares and props. Travel from square to square as you tell the story.

What a shock!

> **Objective:** To give some reasons why things happen or characters change.
> **What you need:** Copies of *The Snail and the Whale*, coloured fabrics, recycled materials, story-linked 'small-world' resources such as snails, a whale, a fire engine.

What to do
● Read the story. Discuss how significant events determine what happens next and the way characters think or feel. For instance, consider why the snails say that the tiny snail has grown when she returns from her travels. Is it because she has been away a long time or is it because her confidence has grown?
● Invite groups of children to re-enact significant story events, for example, create the *smooth black rock* from boxes draped in black shiny fabric and sit ten model snails on it. Re-enact the conversation

among the snails. Question why the tiny snail leaves the rock.
● Ask the groups to perform their chosen events for the others. Discuss what happens in each performance and make links to what will happen next.
● Consider alternative scenarios, for example, someone in a hot-air balloon might respond to the tiny snail's message and take her on quite a different journey!

> **Differentiation**
> **For older/more confident learners:** Invite children to create their own stories about the tiny snail, armed with the knowledge that, as authors, they completely control the direction their characters take.
> **For younger/less confident learners:** Set up small-world backgrounds for children to play out the story in their own way.

Plot, character and setting

Changing feelings

Objective: To draw together ideas and information from across a whole text using simple signposts in the text.
What you need: Copies of *The Snail and the Whale*, photocopiable page 18.
Cross-curricular link: PSHE.

What to do
● Read the story before focusing on the changing feelings of the snail, for example, ask the children how they think she is feeling as the story starts. Re-read the first two pages for clues in the text and illustrations. Write any useful words, for example, *itchy foot, gazed at the sea, 'How I long to sail!', 'Don't wriggle', sighed, sniffed*. Discuss how these words indicate that the snail had a restless longing for adventure.
● Follow the story from beginning to end in the same way. Useful words could be collected under appropriate headings, for example, the different settings.
● Explore how the illustrations show the snail's changing moods, for example, as she fearfully clings to the whale in high seas or smiles happily when returning home.
● Follow similar steps in discussing the changing feelings of the whale and the other snails. Ask: *When the tiny snail leaves, are the other snails glad that she is leaving them in peace or do they feel like joining her? When she returns, are they overjoyed to see their friend again or worried that their peaceful existence will be shattered?*
● Display the photocopiable sheet. Work through this together before providing each child with a copy to complete.

Differentiation
For older/more confident learners: Ask children to work in pairs, thinking of their own 'true' and 'not true' sentences to give to one another to complete.
For younger/less confident learners: Modify adjectives used to suit the level of understanding of individuals.

Happily ever after

Objective: To draw on knowledge and experience of texts in deciding what and how to write.
What you need: Copies of *The Snail and the Whale*.
Cross-curricular link: PSHE.

What to do
● Read the story and then focus on the last two double-page spreads. Talk about how the author uses words effectively to draw the story to a satisfying conclusion, for example, *their wonderful tale, saved the life, they sang to the sea as they all set sail*.
● Explore the idea of a tiny snail saving the life of a huge whale and make links to the traditional tale, 'The Lion and the Mouse'. Explain the moral of both stories. (That kindness has rewards and that no creature is too small to help another, however large.)
● Invite the children to think of different endings to the story by posing the question *What if…?*, for example, *What if the snail decided to stay in a far-off land?*
● Ask the children to write their alternative endings in sentences and read them to the rest of the class.
● Discuss the endings, considering which ones are most effective and why.

Differentiation
For older/more confident children: Invite children to write alternative endings to other stories by the same author, such as *The Gruffalo*.
For younger/less confident children: Read stories with predictable story language, such as 'And they all lived happily ever after'. Encourage children to join in so that they experience this language and the satisfaction of a happy ending.

SECTION 4

When did that happen?

● Cut out the nine sentences in the boxes and arrange them in the correct order to tell the story.

✂

| The whale lost his way and got stuck on the shore. |

| The tide came in and the whale and the snail travelled away. |

| The whale carried the snail on his tail to far-off lands. |

| Once upon a time a tiny snail sat on a rock wishing that she could sail out to sea. |

| All of the snails climbed onto the tail of the whale and set sail. |

| The children asked the firemen to help to keep the whale cool. |

| The snail made a trail on the rock, asking for a lift around the world. |

| The whale and the snail told the other snails all about their adventures. |

| The snail asked the schoolchildren to help to save the whale. |

The snail with the itchy foot

● Colour this picture of the tiny snail. Use the words to label the different parts of the snail's body.

shell

eye

mouth

tentacle

foot

● Colour in the boxes that describe the tiny snail's character.

mean	unkind	brave	angry	fearless
adventurous	helpful	happy	restless	cruel
itchy foot	cheeky	friendly	wicked	scared

● Write a sentence about the tiny snail using some of the words you have read and talked about.

_____

_____

Illustration © 2011, Paul Hutchinson.

READ & RESPOND: Activities based on *The Snail and the Whale*

The journey

- Fill in the missing words to show the journey that the whale and the snail took and the order in which it happened. The words you need are at the bottom of the page.

The whale and the _____ sailed away.

They sailed to _____ lands.

They sailed over high _____.

They sailed to _____ lands.

They sailed under the _____.

They sailed through a _____.

They got _____ in a bay.

They sailed back _____.

The _____ came in.

stuck	sea	cold	home	hot	snail	waves	storm	tide

Changing feelings

● Decide whether each of the sentences below is 'true' or 'not true' and then colour in the correct circle.

The tiny snail was feeling restless when she wanted a lift around the world. (True)　(Not true)
As the tiny snail gazed around her at the sky, the sea and the land she felt big. (True)　(Not true)
As she clung to the whale's tail in the high seas, the tiny snail felt relaxed. (True)　(Not true)
The roar of the speedboats made the whale feel upset. (True)　(Not true)
When the snail saw her friend stuck in the sand she felt helpless. (True)　(Not true)
When the children saw the whale they felt pleased because he was stuck. (True)　(Not true)
At the end of the story the snails felt so sad that they started to sing. (True)　(Not true)

▲SCHOLASTIC
www.scholastic.co.uk

Talk about it

A big problem

Objective: To visualise and comment on events, characters and ideas, making imaginative links to their own experiences.
What you need: Copies of *The Snail and the Whale*, yellow fabric, soft toy whale (or black cushion and table-tennis balls), spades, buckets, watering cans, parasols, firemen's helmets, hose pipes, fans.
Cross-curricular link: PSHE.

What to do

● Sit around a yellow fabric 'beach' with a soft toy whale (or some black cushions with two table-tennis ball eyes!) in the middle. Read the section of *The Snail and the Whale* describing what happens when the whale becomes beached.
● Discuss why being stuck is a problem for the whale. What will happen if he is not kept cool and damp?
● Talk about what the children do when they feel hot in the sun, for example, find shade, have a cold drink, go for a paddle.
● Introduce the suggested resources and discuss how they might solve the whale's problem.
● Ask the children to discuss, in groups, which resource they would choose to keep the whale cool and why, and to prepare a demonstration of how they would do this.
● Bring the class together for the demonstrations and to talk about the most interesting solutions to the whale's problem.

Differentiation
For older/more confident learners: Encourage pairs of children to invent a short dialogue between two firemen at the scene.
For younger/less confident learners: Maroon model whales in a sandtray and find ways to keep them cool, for example, sprinkling them with water or fanning them.

Helping one another

Objective: To tell stories and describe incidents from their own experience in an audible voice.
What you need: Copies of *The Snail and the Whale*, photocopiable page 22.
Cross-curricular link: PSHE.

What to do

● Read the story and then discuss the friendship that grew between the two characters. Consider whether they were friends before the story started. Explore incidents in the story that might have helped the friendship of these two characters to grow.
● Talk about the special qualities of our friends and how friends help and support one another. Focus on the ways that the snail and the whale played this role, enabling each other to achieve a dream and to overcome danger.
● Display the photocopiable sheet and choose two children to read the parts of the snail and the whale. Afterwards, discuss how friends are kind, loyal and considerate, for example, talking about how the gentle whale held the snail clear of the dangerous waves and how the loyal snail went to get help when her friend was in danger.
● Provide copies of the photocopiable sheet so that pairs of children can take turns to read the snail's questions while their partner makes up the whale's reply, elaborating on the response given on the page. Invite pairs to perform their versions to the class.

Differentiation
For older/more confident learners: Ask children to introduce a friend to the rest of the class and recount an incident when he/she has been helpful.
For younger/less confident learners: Ask children to talk to an adult about activities they enjoy doing with their friends and how they share resources.

Talk about it

Rollicking rhymes

> **Objective:** To explore the effects of patterns of language and repeated words and phrases.
> **What you need:** Copies of *The Snail and the Whale*, photocopiable page 23, scissors.
> **Cross-curricular link:** Music.

What to do

● Identify the two rhyming words in the title *The Snail and the Whale*. Ask the children what this might tell us about the story.

● Read the whole story, encouraging the children to listen to the rhythmic lilt which rolls the story along at a satisfying pace. Emphasise this by focusing on a single passage, for example, the page beginning *'This is the sea, So wild and free'*. Ask the children to join in and clap the rhythm.

● Say a pair of rhyming words and then substitute one of them with a non-rhyming word, for example, 'land/sand', 'land/beach', to emphasise the satisfying effect of rhyme.

● Display the photocopiable sheet and explain that the words are from the story. Find the rhyming words together and highlight each point in a different colour.

● Discuss how sounds can be the same but spellings may be different, for example, 'high' and 'sky'. Identify words with matching and then differing letter combinations.

● Give the children the photocopiable sheet to complete.

> **Differentiation**
> **For older/more confident learners:** Suggest that children use the pairs of words created from the photocopiable sheet in new rhyming sentences.
> **For younger/less confident learners:** Read passages from other books by the same author and experience the exciting effect of rhyme together.

The flock on the rock

> **Objective:** To explore familiar themes and characters through improvisation and role play.
> **What you need:** Copies of *The Snail and the Whale*, cushions, black sheets.
> **Cross-curricular links:** PSHE, drama.

What to do

● Explore the page showing the snails on the smooth black rock at the start of the story and read their words together.

● Discuss the snails' mood as they become increasingly irritated by the tiny snail. Contrast their mood with that of the tiny snail as she becomes more and more restless.

● Create large black 'rocks' by covering piles of cushions with black sheets. Invite groups of children to sit on the rocks, pretending to be the snails. Ask them to choose someone in each group to play the tiny snail.

● Encourage the 'snails' to elaborate on their mood, for example, 'I feel really cross with that snail, fussing and fumbling around on our rock. How I wish she would stay in one place like the rest of us.' Ask the 'tiny snail' to respond, for example, 'I want to leave this boring old rock and see the world. That is why I'm sighing and sniffing!'

● Come together as a class to discuss how improvising and role play help us to understand characters.

> **Differentiation**
> **For older/more confident learners:** Invite children to improvise conversations between the snails based on the final pages of the story.
> **For younger/less confident learners:** Take on a 'snail' role to encourage verbal interaction between characters.

Talk about it

Sounds the same

> **Objective:** To spell with increasing accuracy and confidence, drawing on word recognition and knowledge of word structure and spelling patterns including common inflections and use of double letters.
> **What you need:** Copies of *The Snail and the Whale,* photocopiable page 24.

What to do
● Read the story and recall previous discussions about rhyme. Find examples in the book and on the photocopiable sheet of rhyming words that end with the same sounds (phonemes) but have different ways of spelling these sounds (graphemes), for example, 'roar/shore'.
● Write on the board 'In this **tale**, the snail rides on the **tail** of the whale.' Highlight the words 'tale' and 'tail' and ask the children what they notice about them. (They sound like the same word but have a different spelling and meaning.)
● Give examples of words that sound like those in the book but which have different meanings, for example, 'sighed/side'.
● Display the photocopiable sheet and work through it together, highlighting the correct word in each sentence and reinforcing the spelling.
● Provide the children with individual copies of the photocopiable sheet to complete.

> **Differentiation**
> **For older/more confident learners:** Invite the children to make up sentences containing the words that they did not circle when they completed the photocopiable sheet.
> **For younger/less confident learners:** Create a simpler alternative of the photocopiable page, choosing words with graphemes at an appropriate level.

Don't forget about me!

> **Objective:** To tell real and imagined stories using the conventions of familiar story language.
> **What you need:** Copies of *The Snail and the Whale.*
> **Cross-curricular link:** PSHE.

What to do
● Ask the children to name other characters in the story apart from the snail and the whale, for example, the snails on the rock and the schoolchildren. Write up a list of them.
● Go through the book together, ticking off characters already on the list and adding any not mentioned.
● Talk about the importance of these characters. Are they just onlookers or do they play a small part in shaping the story?
● Invite someone to choose a character from the list, for example, the teacher. Together, make up a version of the story from the teacher's viewpoint.

Ask: *How did she feel when a snail started writing a silvery trail on her board? What happened to her class? What might she do then?*
● Ask each child to think of their own version of the story, choosing someone from the list as their main character. Encourage the use of conventional story language, for example, 'Once upon a time…', 'Once there lived a…', '…happily ever after'.
● Divide the children into groups to share their oral stories.

> **Differentiation**
> **For older/more confident learners:** Ask the children to perform their stories in groups to the rest of the class.
> **For younger/less confident learners:** Invite the children to draw a picture of their character and then describe this character to a small group.

Talk about it

Helping one another

● Read this script with a friend. Choose who will be the snail and who will be the whale.

Snail: **Can you help me to see the world?**
Whale: *Yes, I can take you with me as I swim in the sea.*
Snail: **How will you keep me safe, because I cannot swim?**
Whale: *I will carry you high on my tail.*
Snail: **What sort of places will you take me to?**
Whale: *I will take you to far-off lands and golden sands.*
Snail: **Will there be danger?**
Whale: *Only if I get stuck on the sand.*
Snail: **What could I do to help you then?**
Whale: *You could ask people to spray me with water until the tide comes in.*
Snail: **How will that help?**
Whale: *My skin will not dry out before I can swim out to sea again.*

■SCHOLASTIC
www.scholastic.co.uk

READ & RESPOND: Activities based on The Snail and the Whale

Rollicking rhymes

● Read these words and then colour the matching rhymes in the same colour.

snail	roar	fins	rock
bay	school	waves	high
caves	sky	whale	land
flock	small	play	shore
grins	sand	crawl	pool

Sounds the same

● Circle the correct word in the brackets to complete these sentences. Both words sound the same. You must choose the one with the correct spelling and meaning.

This is the (**tale** **tail**) of a tiny snail.

The tiny snail sniffed and (**sighed** **side**) as she sat on the rock.

This is the (**wail** **whale**) who sang to the snail.

The speedboats upset the whale with their loud (**raw** **roar**).

The snail made a silvery trail on the school (**bored** **board**).

The teacher turned (**pail** **pale**) when she saw the snail.

The other snails thought that the snail had (**grown** **groan**) when she came home.

Get writing

My wish…

Objective: To compose and write sentences independently to communicate meaning.
What you need: Copies of *The Snail and the Whale*, sticky notes, wand or stick.
Cross-curricular link: PSHE.

What to do

● Read the story and then focus on the sentence, *'How I long to sail!' said the tiny snail.* Discuss what the snail means by this.

● Show a magic wand and explain that the children can wave it to make one wish come true for the snail. What do they think that wish might be? Talk about their ideas and comment on how closely linked they are to the story.

● Draw two columns, one headed 'The snail's wish' and the other, 'My wish'. Suggest that each child writes their snail's wish on a sticky note and sticks it in the appropriate column.

● Read some of the wishes to the class. Do they reflect the snail's longing?

● Now tell the children that they can wave the wand to make one special wish come true for themselves. Ask them to write the wish down as a sentence and stick it under the 'My wish' heading. Provide a suitable sentence opener for them, for example, 'My special wish is…' or, 'If I could have one special wish it would be…'.

● Discuss the range of children's wishes and make comparisons with those of the snail.

Differentiation
For older/more confident learners: Read traditional stories that centre around three wishes, for example, the Swedish tale, 'The Sausage'. Suggest that children write their own 'Three wish' stories in three sentences.
For younger/less confident learners: Prepare sentence openers, for example, 'I wish I could…' for children to complete in words or pictures.

What is happening?

Objectives: To use capital letters and full stops when punctuating simple sentences. To compose and write sentences independently to communicate meaning.
What you need: Copies of *The Snail and the Whale*, photocopiable page 28.

What to do

● Explore the illustrations depicting the firemen and schoolchildren trying to keep the whale cool. Talk about how illustrations include extra detail that we cannot learn from the text, for example, where the water in the hoses came from.

● Discuss what people might be saying to one another, for example, the fireman pointing at the whale and talking to the fireman on the ladder. Encourage the children to use full sentences when suggesting ideas for this dialogue.

● Discuss what people are doing, for example, the little boy who is holding the tiny snail so

carefully on both pages. Again, encourage the use of full sentences in oral responses.

● Display the photocopiable sheet. Explain that it is like a puzzle because the children have to search the story for tiny details. Read each question together, giving support with challenging words such as 'ginger' and 'penguin'.

● Ask the children to work in groups to search the story for answers to the questions on the photocopiable sheet.

● Give each child a copy of the photocopiable sheet to complete.

Differentiation
For older/more confident learners: Invite children to make up questions of their own for the class to answer, based on detail in the illustrations.
For younger/less confident learners: Simplify the words used to suit individual reading levels, for example, 'Where is the bell?'.

Get writing

Information detectives

Objective: To convey information and ideas in simple non-narrative forms.
What you need: Copies of *The Snail and the Whale*, access to books and websites about transport, paper, drawing materials.
Cross-curricular links: ICT, geography.

What to do

- Talk about where we can find more information about the types of transport featured in the story, for example, by interviewing experts, reading books, searching the internet, visiting actual locations.
- Establish that the starting point will be to list the types of transport in the book, such as liner, trawler, cargo ship, speedboat, helicopter, fire engine. Ask the children to work in pairs to make these lists, double-checking in the book afterwards if they need to.
- Ask the children, still in their pairs, to search for and note down interesting facts for the types of transport on their lists, using some of the sources of information discussed. Suggest headings such as 'What is it used for?', 'How does it move?', 'What size is it?'. If necessary, work through examples with any pairs to support their understanding of note-taking.
- Suggest that each pair draws a picture of one of the featured forms of transport and then writes information from their notes underneath.
- Bring the class together to present findings.

Differentiation
For older/more confident learners: Invite children to investigate another item of interest in the book in this way, for example, underwater creatures.
For younger/less confident learners: Focus on a favourite form of transport featured, for example, fire engines. Ask the children to search picture books for information, draw a picture and write a simple sentence.

Thank you, my friend!

Objective: To select from different presentational features to suit particular purposes on paper and on screen.
What you need: Copies of *The Snail and the Whale*, wallpaper rolls, drawing and colouring materials, string, tape.
Cross-curricular links: Design and technology, PSHE.

What to do

- Read *The Snail and the Whale* and extend the story by making up a conversation between the tiny snail and the other snails when she tells them that she has forgotten to say 'Thank you' for the whale's help.
- Discuss the children's experiences of saying 'Thank you' to someone, perhaps verbally or by sending a card or gift.
- Pose the question of how the snail might still thank the whale. Perhaps she could make a huge 'Thank you' banner or flag, but where would she hang it to be sure that the whale would notice it? (On the side of a lighthouse, ship or rock? Tied to a helicopter?)
- Divide the children into groups. Provide resources to make and decorate 'Thank you' banners which should include a simple, written message such as 'Thank you for my trip'.
- Use string and tape to suspend the banners around the room.

Differentiation
For older/more confident learners: Ask the children to write 'Thank you' letters from the snail to the whale to be delivered by a passing fishing boat.
For younger/less confident learners: Invite children to **help** an adult to make an illustrated paper banner, collaging the words 'Thank you'.

Get writing

Stringing along

Objective: To spell with increasing accuracy and confidence, drawing on word recognition and knowledge of word structure and spelling patterns including common inflections and double letters.
What you need: Copies of *The Snail and the Whale*, photocopiable page 29, chalk.
Cross-curricular link: Music.

What to do

● Read the story and recall discussions about rhyme and rhythm.
● Together, chant rhyming words from two successive lines, for example, *race, place, race, place*. Clap the rhythm at the same time. Vary the sound pattern by emphasising the first word of each pair and then the second (*race, place, **race**, place*, then *race, **place**, race, **place***).
● Ask individuals to write words such as 'lace' and 'face' on the board to continue the string.
● Go outside and, together, stamp out the rhythm of the children's rhyming strings, placing emphasis on different words by stamping harder with one foot.
● Draw a wiggly chalk line around the play-ground representing the snail's *silvery trail*. Hold onto one another like a train, chanting and stamping the rhyming strings as you go along the trail.
● Ask children to write words on the ground to form rhyming strings, and jump from word to word while chanting.
● Give each child a copy of the photocopiable page to complete.

Differentiation
For older/more confident learners: Challenge children to read and write strings with differing graphemes, for example, 'sky', 'high', 'pie'.
For younger/less confident learners: Involve children in writing simple CVC strings, for example, 'pot', 'hot', 'cot'.

Book review

Objective: To explain their reactions to texts, commenting on important aspects.
What you need: Copies of *The Snail and the Whale*, photocopiable page 30.

What to do

● Invite children to give their overall impressions of the story. Ask them what they enjoyed most about the book. Discuss their opinions of the illustrations. Question them as to whether the regular rhyme added to their enjoyment or not.
● Explain the purpose of a book review and read sample reviews from the backs of the children's favourite books. Suggest that the children write their own reviews of *The Snail and the Whale*.
● Display the photocopiable sheet and read it together, a section at a time. Discuss how the individual settings are linked because they are in and around the sea. Decide whether this is a suitable place to set a story. Talk about the merits or possible shortcomings of characters, events and illustrations. If necessary, explain the star rating system.
● Give each child a copy of the photocopiable sheet to use as a plan prior to writing an independent book review.

Differentiation
For older/more confident learners: Invite children to choose a different story to review, using the same approach.
For younger/less confident learners: Focus on reviewing a favourite event in the book, for example, when the whale was stuck on the beach. Ask children to draw a picture and write about their feelings on the event.

Get writing

What is happening?

● Answer the questions by looking closely at the pictures in the book. Remember to write in sentences starting with a capital letter and ending with a full stop.

What is the ginger cat on the harbour wall looking at?
What are the penguins doing?
Where is the lobster hiding?
What do you think the two crabs are doing?
What is the little boy drawing in the sand?
Who is carrying the tiny snail from the school to the beach?

Stringing along

● Continue these rhyming strings by adding words of your own.

dock	clock		
whale	tale		
bright	night		
brave	wave		
small	ball		
grand	band		
crash	dash		

READ & RESPOND: Activities based on The Snail and the Whale

Book review

● Use this page to help you to plan and write a book review for *The Snail and the Whale*. Finish the sentences in the boxes, giving your opinions.

The settings: I think that setting a story near or in the sea is good

because _____

_____

The characters: I like the character of the tiny snail because

_____

I think the whale is _____

Events: My favourite story event is

_____

A story event I would change is

_____

Rhyme: I think that the rhymes make this book

_____

My favourite rhyming words are

_____

Illustrations: I think the illustrations are important in this book

because _____

_____

My rating: Give the story a rating out of five by shading the stars.

☆ ☆ ☆ ☆ ☆

Assessment

Assessment advice

Ongoing formative assessments of individual achievements and progress in literacy are an essential component of the planning and assessment cycle. They help you to make valuable judgements about a child's progress towards specific learning targets and provide supportive evidence when planning appropriate future learning activities and when setting new targets.

Formative assessments build up gradually and should be based on various sources including observations, contributions to class and group discussions, actual completed work, and analysis of practical tasks. The importance of peer and self-assessment should not be underestimated and the activities in this book can be assessed in both these ways.

Each activity in the book has a clear, assessable learning objective which represents what a child should know, or be able to do, by the end of that activity. Informing children of these objectives before an activity begins will highlight for them their involvement in their own learning. At the end of each activity there should be time for reflection, when children can revisit the learning objective and discuss whether or not they think they have achieved it. This helps them to recognise the relevance of assessment in planning the next steps in learning.

You can use photocopiable page 32 as part of a record of individual progress. It is also a useful tool for assessing a child's ability to plan and write a story on a given theme.

A shared adventure

> **Assessment focus:** To independently choose what to write about, plan and follow it through.
> **What you need:** Copies of *The Snail and the Whale*, photocopiable page 32.

What to do
● Discuss the adventure that the two characters shared. Talk about the events that happened and the ultimate outcome.
● Invite the children to invent two main characters of their own and to make up a story about a shared adventure. Allow time for children to discuss their initial ideas with one another.
● Display the photocopiable sheet and read through it together. Using one of your ideas as an example, fill in the boxes together.
● Provide each child with a copy of the photocopiable sheet to plan their story. As the children are planning, interact with individuals to support their ideas. Encourage them to focus on the story structure, with appropriate opening and closing words and a brief description of two of the main events. Promote inventiveness in their character descriptions and interactions.
● Invite children to write out their stories in full, referring to their written plans.
● Bring the class together to comment on the finished stories. Encourage the children to talk about those things they feel work well and also to suggest improvements.

A shared adventure

● Use this sheet to plan your own story about an adventure shared by two friends.

Title:_____

Main character 1:_____

Main character 2:_____

Setting: _____

Beginning

Make a note of words you are going to use to begin your story.

_____

_____

Middle

Make a note of two main events in the story.

1._____

2._____

End

Make a note of words you could use to end your story.

_____

_____

_____